T0340524

Singing

SPANISH

22 PHOTOCOPIABLE SONGS AND CHANTS FOR LEARNING SPANISH

HELEN MACGREGOR &
STEPHEN CHADWICK

Contents

Published by Collins
An imprint of HarperCollins*Publishers* Ltd
The News Building
1 London Bridge Street
London
SE1 9GF

HarperCollins*Publishers*
Macken House
39/40 Mayor Street Upper
Dublin 1, D01 C9W8
Ireland

3

Copyright © Helen MacGregor and Stephen Chadwick 2008
Audio © HarperCollins*Publishers* Ltd 2008

ISBN 978-0-7136-8880-1
Edited by Lucy Poddington and Emily Wilson
Designed by Jocelyn Lucas
Cover illustration © E. E. Harding 2008
Inside illustrations © Joy Gosney 2008
Audio produced by Stephen Chadwick at 3D Music Ltd Performed by
Pablo Castillo and María Romero
Music set by Jeanne Roberts

Printed and bound in the UK using 100%
Renewable Electricity at CPI Group (UK) Ltd

A CIP catalogue record for this book is available from the British Library.

This book is produced from independently certified FSC™
paper to ensure responsible forest management.

For more information visit: www.harpercollins.co.uk/green

Introduction

Singing Spanish is an exciting new collection of songs and chants which supports the teaching of Spanish to beginners. It is intended for Spanish teachers and parents with Spanish language of any level.

The audio comprises performance tracks sung by native Spanish speakers and backing tracks for every song, as well as teaching tracks for some of the songs giving spoken pronunciation reference for key vocabulary. The book contains photocopiable song words for each song and teaching ideas which develop children's abilities to communicate in Spanish and to appreciate Spanish culture. No music reading is required to use the resource. However, melody lines are provided at the back of the book for music readers.

The resource links closely with the Qualifications and Curriculum Authority (QCA) guidelines and scheme of work for teaching Modern Foreign Languages (MFL) in primary, middle and special schools at Key Stage Two. It can also be used to support Spanish teaching at Key Stage Three for pupils who have had little or no prior teaching of the language. The resource may be used alongside any scheme of work.

The songs and activity ideas in **Singing Spanish** help children to:

- enjoy and become familiar with the sounds of the Spanish language;

- develop language skills and language-learning skills;

- become confident in speaking, understanding and reading a new language;

- learn about Spanish culture and people.

Using the songs

Each song links to one or more aspects of language content from the QCA MFL scheme of work. The songs can be taught in any order to complement your teaching, but are arranged progressively in the book, with the later songs building on vocabulary already learnt and containing less repetition of words and phrases.

To familiarise children with the sounds of the Spanish language and to develop good listening and aural memory skills, it is generally advisable to teach the songs using the audio or by singing them yourself before introducing the children to the written words. Singing the songs without the support of the audio enables you to adapt the pitch and tempo of each song to suit the particular needs of your children. It is important to revisit the songs with sufficient frequency over a period of time for the children to become confident with the language.

The track numbers are referred to at appropriate points throughout the teaching notes and a full track list can be found on page 64. You will find teaching tracks giving pronunciation guidance for key words and phrases from the later songs. These can be used when teaching the song vocabulary. You can download the audio from collins.co.uk/singing-downloads.

Guidance is given for each of the songs about possible ways of teaching and performing them, for example:

- by joining in with key phrases or the chorus on first listening, then gradually learning the whole song;

- by performing in two groups;

- by inviting smaller groups or soloists to perform parts.

The resource is designed to be used flexibly so that you can adapt the songs and activities to cater for the age, ability and experience of the children.

Once the songs have been learnt, they can be sung regularly at any time, either with the backing track or unaccompanied. Many songs lend themselves to adding actions, dance steps and/or percussion accompaniments, and could be incorporated into music lessons. There are many opportunities suggested in the teaching notes for the children to develop the songs by writing their own verses. Performances could be recorded for discussion and evaluation.

Developing the vocabulary

For each song, ideas are provided of ways to extend learning using the song vocabulary as a starting point. These activities may be completed at the same time as learning the song or may be used at a later stage. Often the children are asked to compose their own song words to perform with the backing track, offering opportunities for differentiation and independent learning.

Key vocabulary for each song is given in the vocabulary box, with translations. The children could be encouraged to research further vocabulary using dictionaries.

Follow-up work

Linked to each song are suggestions for games, role plays, research projects and cross-curricular activities to further the children's knowledge of Spanish language and culture. These activities often involve combining vocabulary from a range of topics.

Many of the follow-up ideas can be used as extension activities for the more confident pupils, either working individually or in small groups. Other suggestions are suitable for use with the whole class, perhaps at a later stage, to consolidate and extend their learning. The activities incorporate reading, writing and use of ICT, and make other cross-curricular links with subjects such as geography, PSHE and citizenship.

Photocopiable song words

When the children are able to sing a song confidently (or at a later stage), you can introduce them to the written song words on the photocopiable song sheets. These can be used in a variety of ways to support the development of literacy in the language. For example, the sheet could be:

- displayed as a song sheet on an OHT or interactive whiteboard;

- enlarged and displayed on the classroom wall as a poster;

- used in a lesson focusing on reading and writing;

- presented as a stimulus for composing new song words.

Resources

Few additional resources are required in order to learn the songs and use the teaching ideas. Many of the illustrations on the photocopiable song sheets can be enlarged to make lively visual aids. Photocopiable number cards for use when learning numbers can be found on page 63. **Please note that any material not marked 'photocopiable' may not be photocopied.**

When using the suggestions for developing the vocabulary and follow-up work, try to ensure that the children have access to Spanish–English dictionaries so that they can look up additional vocabulary.

Once the songs have been learnt, they can easily be performed unaccompanied if you cannot play the audio.

Melody lines

Melody lines are provided at the back of the book for music readers. Teachers or pupils may wish to play the melody lines on a piano, keyboard or other pitched instrument when composing new song words.

Pronunciation

Spanish is a phonetic language: once mastered, each letter or combination of letters is always pronounced the same. Many letter sounds are similar to those in the English language.

Spanish words of more than one syllable are spoken with different stresses, eg in **co-lor, na-dar, ju-gar**, the stress is on the second syllable, but in **rí-o, fút-bol, mú-si-ca** the stress is on the first syllable (indicated by the accent). In words of more syllables the stress is usually on the penultimate syllable, eg **pri-ma-ve-ra, cum-ple-a-ños**.

Care has been taken to retain the natural stresses of spoken Spanish in the musical rhythms of the melodies, so that children learn this as an intrinsic part of becoming familiar with the vocabulary through the songs.

Diphthongs (blended vowel sounds) should be spoken as one syllable, eg **diez** and **cien** are single-syllable words and **bue-nos** and **gra-cias** each have two syllables, not three. This is modelled by the rhythms of the song melodies.

Hola

greetings/introducing yourself

Using the song

All listen to the song (track 1). Ask the children if they can identify the four Spanish girls' names they hear (María, Elena, Teresa, Camila) and the four boys' names (Fernando, Guillermo, Antonio, Matías). Teach the phrases either using track 1 or by saying the words yourself for the children to copy.

Divide the class according to gender to sing the song with track 1, the girls joining in with the female voice in the first half and the boys singing with the male voice in the second half.

When the class is familiar with the whole song, sing it in two parts with the backing track (track 2), inviting confident individuals to respond to the questions by introducing themselves.

key vocabulary

¡Hola! – Hello!

(Yo) me llamo ... – My name is ...

¿Cómo te llamas? – What is your name?

¿Y tú? – And you?

Developing the vocabulary

Write the greeting **¡Hola!** on the board and explain that when an exclamation mark is used in Spanish, it appears upside down at the beginning of the word or phrase as well as at the end in the usual way. The same applies to question marks.

Tell the children that they are going to practise introducing themselves in Spanish. Move around the room shaking hands with individual children, introducing yourself and inviting them to respond, eg

¡Hola! Me llamo Helen. ¿Cómo te llamas?

Teach the phrases **Éste es** and **Ésta es** (this is, m/f) by pointing to individual children and naming them, eg

Éste es Daniel. Ésta es Sophie.

Ask the children what they notice about the phrases, drawing out that they are different depending on whether you are introducing a boy or girl.

Divide the children into small groups and ask them to form a circle. Each child introduces him- or herself and then the child to their left, eg

Madison: **¡Hola! Me llamo Madison. Éste es Tom.**

Tom: **¡Hola! Me llamo Tom. Ésta es Saima.**

When the children have completed their introductions around the circle, they may change places and repeat the game. Invite each group to demonstrate their introductions to the class.

Follow-up work

Take the daily register in Spanish. Teach the children to respond by saying **presente** (present) or by naming children who are absent, eg

Kyle está ausente. (Kyle is absent.)

If everyone is present, use the phrase **Toda la clase está presente**.

Invite individuals to greet the class in Spanish and take the register.

Once topics such as family, clothing and hobbies have been introduced, give the children opportunities to introduce and describe themselves in further detail, eg

¡Hola! Me llamo Lucy. Tengo diez años. Tengo dos hermanos. Yo nado bien.

(Hello. My name is Lucy. I'm ten years old. I have two brothers. I'm good at swimming.)

Hola

¡Hola! ¡Hola! Me llamo María.
¡Hola! ¡Hola! Me llamo Elena.
¡Hola! ¡Hola! Me llamo Teresa.
¡Hola! ¡Hola! Me llamo Camila.

¿Cómo te llamas?
☺ Me llamo ....
¿Cómo te llamas?
☺ Me llamo ....
¿Cómo te llamas?
☺ Me llamo ....
¿Y tú?
☺ Me llamo ....

¡Hola! ¡Hola! Me llamo Fernando.
¡Hola! ¡Hola! Me llamo Guillermo.
¡Hola! ¡Hola! Me llamo Antonio.
¡Hola! ¡Hola! Me llamo Matías.

¿Cómo te llamas?
☺ Me llamo ....
¿Cómo te llamas?
☺ Me llamo ....
¿Cómo te llamas?
☺ Me llamo ....
¿Y tú?
☺ Me llamo ....

photocopiable

Buenos días

greetings/asking how someone is

Using the song

All listen to the song (track 3). During the first two verses, approach individual children and shake their hands. Wave goodbye during the last verse. Ask the children if they can tell you the meaning of the words **Hola** and **Adiós**. Listen to the song again, all joining in with **¡Hola!** and **¡Adiós!**

Teach the children the exclamations and question in the song:

¡Buenos días! ¡Buenas tardes! ¡Buenas noches!
¿Qué tal?   ¡Chao!

Play track 3 again and all join in with these phrases.

Teach the vocabulary **Estoy bien, muy bien, gracias** by listening to track 3 or by saying the words yourself for the children to copy. Finally, learn the remainder of the last verse line by line. When the class is familiar with the whole song, sing it with the backing track (track 4).

You may like to perform the song in two groups, allocating the greeting sections to one group and the reply sections to the other. Then swap parts.

Developing the vocabulary

Using the backing track (track 4), sing the part of the leader (shown in bold on the photocopiable song sheet), choosing the name of a child to substitute for the word **¡Hola!** The chosen child sings the response. The whole class joins in with the last verse.

Introduce **¿Cómo estás?** as an alternative to **¿Qué tal?** (How are you?), then teach further vocabulary for replying, eg

Genial/Estoy genial. (I'm great.)

Así así. (So-so.)

Mal/Estoy mal. (I'm not well.)

Fatal/Estoy fatal. (I feel terrible.)

Encourage the children to follow their answer with **¿Y tú?** (And you?). In pairs, the children can practise using this vocabulary in conversations, taking turns to lead.

Teach the class other ways of saying goodbye:

¡Hasta la vista! (Goodbye!)   **¡Hasta luego!** (See you later!)

¡Hasta mañana! (See you tomorrow!)

key vocabulary

¡Buenos días! – Good morning!

¡Hola! – Hello!

¿Qué tal? – How are you?

Estoy bien – I am well

muy bien – very well

gracias – thank you

¡Buenas tardes! – Good afternoon!

¡Buenas noches! – Good evening/ Goodnight!

¡Adiós! – Goodbye!

¡Chao! – Bye!

mira/mirad – look at (sing/pl)

la luna – the moon

las estrellas (una estrella) – the stars (a star)

Follow-up work

Explain to the children the difference between different forms of greeting: **¡Hola!** and **¿Cómo estás?** are informal, whereas **¡Buenos días!** and **¿Cómo está?** are formal.

Tell the class how to address you as their teacher: **Maestro/Maestra**. Take the register, asking individuals **¿Estás bien?** (Are you well?) to elicit the response **Sí, muy bien, Maestro/ Maestra**.

Also ask the open question **¿Cómo estás?** so that individuals can practise replying with the vocabulary previously learnt.

Invite confident individuals to take the register in the morning or afternoon, pretending to be the teacher as they greet each child and ask how they are, to elicit a response.

Buenos días

¡Buenos días! ¡Hola!
¡Buenos días! ¡Hola!
¡Buenos días! ¡Hola!
¡Buenos días! ¿Qué tal?
Estoy bien, muy bien,
Bien, muy bien.
Estoy bien, muy bien, gracias.

¡Buenas tardes! ¡Hola!
¡Buenas tardes! ¡Hola!
¡Buenas tardes! ¡Hola!
¡Buenas tardes! ¿Qué tal?
Estoy bien, muy bien,
Bien, muy bien.
Estoy bien, muy bien, gracias.

¡Buenas noches! ¡Adiós!
¡Buenas noches! ¡Adiós!
¡Buenas noches! ¡Adiós!
¡Buenas noches! ¡Chao!
Mira la luna, la luna,
La luna, las estrellas.
Mira la luna, la luna. ¡Chao!

¿Cuántos animales?

numbers 1 to 3/animals

Using the song

Listen to the song several times (track 5), then all join in singing the words **uno**, **dos**, **tres** in each verse. As you sing each number, hold up the correct number of fingers or show number cards (see page 63).

Teach the rest of the vocabulary either using the song or by saying the words yourself for the children to copy. Show the class the pictures on the photocopiable song sheet as you say the vocabulary, to reinforce the meaning of the words.

Practise singing the song with track 5, without using the song sheet. When the class is familiar with the whole song, sing it with the backing track (track 6).

Developing the vocabulary

Teach the class the names of other animals and together make up new verses using other animal names, eg

Tengo tres gatos (cats)
Tengo tres peces (fish)
Tengo tres hámsters (hamsters)

All sing the new verses with the backing track (track 6).

Explain to the children that Spanish nouns are either masculine or feminine, eg **un perro** (a dog), **una gallina** (a hen). Almost all nouns ending in 'o' are masculine and most ending in 'a' are feminine.

If you wish, discuss regular and irregular plurals with the class. To make a plural of a noun ending in a vowel, simply add an 's'. For a noun ending in a consonant, add 'es'. Some nouns form irregular plurals, eg **un ratón/tres ratones, un pez/tres peces**.

Teach the class the question **¿Tienes animales en casa?** (Do you have any pets?) and the vocabulary **sí** (yes) and **no** (no). In pairs, the children can practise asking the question and giving an appropriate response, eg

Sí, tengo dos gatos y un hámster. (Yes, I have two cats and a hamster.)
No, no tengo. (No, I don't have any.)

key vocabulary

¿Cuántos? – How many?
los animales (un animal) – animals (an animal)
uno – one
dos – two
tres – three
tengo – I have
tres tortugas (una tortuga) – three tortoises (a tortoise)
tres conejos (un conejo) – three rabbits (a rabbit)
tres perros (un perro) – three dogs (a dog)
tres ratones (un ratón) – three mice (a mouse)
repite/repetid – repeat (sing/pl)

Follow-up work

Once the children have learnt numbers up to ten, make up new verses of the song using other number sequences, eg

¿Cuántos animales?
Cuatro, cinco, seis,
Tengo seis caballos, (horses)
Cuatro, cinco, seis.

Introduce the children to the masculine, feminine and plural forms of the article 'the':

el perro/los perros (the dog/the dogs)
la gallina/las gallinas (the hen/the hens)

Hold up picture cards showing animals previously learnt, both singly and in groups of the same kind. Invite the children to identify them by calling out the singular or plural, eg **el gato, la tortuga, los perros, las gallinas**.

¿Cuántos animales?

¿Cuántos animales?
Uno, dos, tres,
Tengo tres tortugas,
Uno, dos, tres.

¿Cuántos animales?
Uno, dos, tres,
Tengo tres conejos,
Uno, dos, tres.

¿Cuántos animales?
Uno, dos, tres,
Tengo tres perros,
Uno, dos, tres.

¿Cuántos animales?
Uno, dos, tres,
Tengo tres ratones,
Uno, dos, tres.

....
repetid
....

De uno a diez

numbers 1 to 10

Using the song

Enlarge the number cards on page 63 and use them to make a number track from one to ten. Explain to the children that they are going to learn the numbers from one to ten. Listen to the song (track 7), pointing to each number as it occurs in the song.

Sing the song several times until everyone is confident with the vocabulary. You may then like to divide into two groups to sing alternate lines, with both groups joining in with the final number (**diez**). Perform the song with the backing track (track 8), swapping parts in the repeat so that each group has a chance to lead the song.

Developing the vocabulary

When the class is confident with the song, all sit in a circle and sing the song round the circle. Choose a child to start and ask each child to sing one number: Child 1: **Uno**, Child 2: **dos**, Child 3: **tres**, Child 4: **Uno**, Child 5: **dos** ... and so on. This is quite tricky, so start by chanting slowly at first. Then practise it with the backing track (track 8). It will help to ask a confident individual to stand in the middle of the circle and conduct by pointing at the child whose turn it is to sing next.

Introduce the children to the following phrases:

¿Cuántos años tienes? (How old are you?)

Tengo diez años. (I am ten.)

¡Yo también! (Me too!)

If appropriate for the age of your class, teach the numbers **once** (eleven) and **doce** (twelve). Ask the children to form pairs, shake hands and introduce themselves, using these phrases with the greetings vocabulary previously learnt.

key vocabulary

de uno a diez – from one to ten

uno – one

dos – two

tres – three

cuatro – four

cinco – five

seis – six

siete – seven

ocho – eight

nueve – nine

diez – ten

repite/repetid – repeat (sing/pl)

Follow-up work

Make a set of number cards from one to ten using the photocopiable number cards on page 63. Select ten children to stand in a line facing the class. Allocate one card to each child, which they hold up for the class to see.

Invite an individual to put the children in a different order to make a new number sequence, eg

10 9 8 7 3 2 1 6 5 4

As the individual points to each card in turn, the class chants the new number sequence.

To familiarise the class with the written number words, repeat the activity using cards which show the numbers in words and figures. (Alternatively, write the numbers in words and figures on the board.)

De uno a diez

Uno dos tres,
Uno dos tres,
Cuatro cinco seis,
Cuatro cinco seis.

Uno dos tres,
Uno dos tres,
Cuatro cinco seis,
Cuatro cinco seis.
Siete ocho nueve,
Siete ocho nueve,
Diez.

repetid

Campeones
celebrating achievements/saying what you can do well

Using the song

Listen to the song (track 9). Ask the children what they notice about the first four lines, which are repeated as the chorus. (They are sung alternately by female and male singers; the words are almost the same.) Explain the meaning of the first four lines, pointing out the masculine and feminine forms of **un campeón/una campeona**.

Divide the class into two groups according to gender and ask them to join in with the alternating female and male lines of the chorus.

Teach the question and answer sections of the song using track 9 or by saying the words yourself for the children to copy. You could add actions to help convey the meaning of the words. When the children are familiar with the whole song, sing it with the backing track (track 10). You may like to ask smaller groups of children to perform the question and answer sections.

Developing the vocabulary

Teach the class more vocabulary relating to hobbies, eg

bailar/(yo) bailo – to dance/I dance

(yo) bailo bien – I'm good at dancing

saltar/(yo) salto – to jump/I jump

leer/(yo) leo – to read/I read

correr/(yo) corro – to run/I run

Point out that in Spanish verbs the word ending tells you who the subject is, eg the 'o' ending indicates that it is the first person. Explain that the word **yo** ('I') is often missed out in conversation.

Practise the vocabulary as a class or in small groups, using actions to reinforce the meaning of the verbs. As a class, create new question and answer sections for the song, using the new vocabulary, eg

¿Sabes bailar? ¿Bailas bien? Yo sé bailar, bailo bien.

¿Sabes correr? ¿Corres bien? Yo sé correr, corro bien.

key vocabulary

campeones – champions

un campeón/una campeona – a champion/star (m/f)

muy bien – very good

eres – you are

estupendo – wonderful

soy – I am

¿Sabes ...? – Can you/Do you know how to ...?

nadar – to swim

¿Nadas bien? – Are you good at swimming?

(yo) sé – I can/I know how to

(yo) nado bien – I'm good at swimming **cantar** – to sing

¿Cantas bien? – Are you good at singing?

(yo) canto bien – I'm good at singing

jugar al fútbol – to play football

(yo) juego bien – I play well

Follow-up work

When it is appropriate, introduce more forms of regular verbs ending in -ar and -er, eg

(tú) nadas (you swim, sing informal)

(él/ella) nada (he/she swims) **(nosotros/nosotras) nadamos** (we swim, m/f)

(vosotros/vosotras) nadáis (you swim, pl informal, m/f)

(ellos/ellas) nadan (they swim, m/f)

(tú) corres
(él/ella) corre
(nosotros/nosotras) corremos
(vosotros/vosotras) corréis
(ellos/ellas) corren

Encourage the children to use these verb forms in sentences, eg

Ésta es Millie. Corre bien.

Campeones

¡Muy bien, muy bien, eres un campeón!
¡Muy bien, muy bien, eres una campeona!
¡Estupendo, soy un campeón!
¡Estupendo, soy una campeona!

¿Sabes nadar? ¿Nadas bien?
Yo sé nadar, nado bien.

¡Muy bien, muy bien, eres un campeón! ...

¿Sabes cantar? ¿Cantas bien?
Yo sé cantar, canto bien.

¡Muy bien, muy bien, eres un campeón! ...

¿Sabes jugar, jugar al fútbol?
Yo sé jugar, juego bien.

¡Muy bien, muy bien, eres un campeón! ...

SINGING SPANISH © HELEN MACGREGOR & STEPHEN CHADWICK 2008, HarperCollins*Publishers* Ltd

Mi color favorito

colours/expressing likes and dislikes

Using the song

Before the lesson prepare a set of coloured cards, one for each of the six colours referred to in the song. Tell the children they are going to hear a song about colours. Then play track 11, holding up each card as the name of the colour is heard. Ask the children if they can guess the meaning of the phrases **mi color favorito es**, **y me gusta** and **no me gusta**.

To reinforce the names of the colours, you could play **Sí/No** (Yes/No) with the class. Hold up a card and name a colour. If the named colour matches the card the children shout **¡Sí!** If the colour does not match they shout **¡No!** You could invite confident children to take turns in leading the game.

When the children are confident at recognising the colours aurally, invite six children to the front of the class to hold up the colour cards at the appropriate places in the song. Play track 11 again, all joining in with the names of the colours.

Gradually learn the whole song to sing with the backing track (track 12).

key vocabulary

mi color favorito – my favourite colour

es – is

(el) rosa – pink

y – and

me gusta – I like

(el) azul – blue

(el) blanco – white

(el) rojo – red

(el) verde – green

(el) marrón – brown

no me gusta – I don't like

Developing the vocabulary

Teach the children the alternative vocabulary **mi color preferido** and sing the song with the backing track (track 12), using this phrase in place of **mi color favorito**.

Teach the vocabulary for more colours, eg

(el) amarillo (yellow) **(el) violeta** (purple) **(el) naranja** (orange)
(el) gris (grey) **(el) negro** (black)

The children can make up new verses individually, choosing their favourite colour and another colour that they like or dislike. In pairs, each child should sing or say their verse to their partner who identifies the colours and preferences.

Teach the class the question **¿Te gusta ...?** (Do you like ...?) and the responses **Sí, me gusta ...** (Yes, I like ...) / **No, no me gusta ... Prefiero ...** (No, I don't like ... I prefer ...). Then ask individuals about their colour preferences, eg

¿Thomas, te gusta el rojo?

Follow-up work

Explain to the class that when colours are used as adjectives they do not need the article (**el/la**), eg **un gato blanco** (a white cat).

When the children are familiar with the vocabulary for parts of the body, tell them about the agreement of nouns and adjectives and invite them to describe themselves, eg

Tengo los ojos azules. (I have blue eyes.)

Ask the children each to draw a monster and colour in the body parts. Invite the 'monsters' to describe themselves to the class, eg

Tengo el pelo verde, los pies rosas y la nariz amarilla.
(I have green hair, pink feet and a yellow nose.)

Any children with matching colours should stand up and point to the appropriate part of their body.

Mi color favorito

Mi color favorito es el rosa, rosa,
Y me gusta el azul.

Mi color favorito es el azul, azul,
Y me gusta el blanco.

Rosa, rosa, rosa,
Azul, azul, azul,
Blanco, blanco, blanco,
Rojo, rojo, rojo, verde, marrón.

Mi color favorito es el blanco, blanco,
Y me gusta el rojo.

Mi color favorito es el rojo, rojo,
Y me gusta el verde.

Rosa, rosa, rosa,
Azul, azul, azul,
Blanco, blanco, blanco,
Rojo, rojo, rojo, verde, marrón.

Mi color favorito es el verde, verde,
No me gusta el marrón.

photocopiable

El cuerpo

parts of the body

Tracks   **13** the song   **14** backing track   **45** spoken phrases

Using the song

Listen to the song (track 13), pointing to the appropriate parts of your body during the verses and encouraging the children to copy you. Ask them to identify any vocabulary they recognise, such as numbers or colours.

Teach the children the chorus line by line using track 45 or by saying the phrases yourself for the children to copy. Ensure that they understand the words, then listen to the song again and all join in with the chorus. Teach the remaining vocabulary by indicating each part of the body and naming it for the class to copy. Demonstrate exaggerated actions to match the

adjectives **grandes**, **pequeñas/pequeños**, **largos** and **fuertes**, asking the children to copy you.

When everyone is familiar with the vocabulary, learn to sing the verses one at a time using track 13. Finally, sing the song all the way through with the backing track (track 14), performing the actions as you sing.

Developing the vocabulary

Introduce vocabulary for other parts of the body, eg

la cabeza (the head)   **la mano** (the hand)

el pelo (hair)   **el pie** (the foot)

las rodillas/una rodilla (knees)

Extend the vocabulary gradually to create new verses to sing with the backing track (track 14), eg

Tengo el pelo corto,	(I have short hair,)
Corto y rizado.	(Short and curly.)
Tengo el pelo corto	(I have short hair)
En mi cabeza, cabeza.	(On my head.)

Teach the word **tocad** (touch – plural). Play **Simón dice** (Simon says): ask the children to touch a part of their body, starting with the words **Simón dice**, eg

Simón dice: tocad la cabeza. (Simon says: touch the head.)

Simón dice: tocad los ojos. (Simon says: touch the eyes.)

If the words **Simón dice** are omitted, eg **Tocad la cabeza**, the children must ignore the instruction. When they make a mistake they are 'out' of the game.

key vocabulary

el cuerpo – the body

todos somos diferentes – everyone's different

el cuerpo humano – the human body

es – is

magnífico – wonderful

(yo) tengo – I have

dos – two

los ojos (un ojo) – eyes (one eye) **grande** – big

y – and

una nariz – a nose/one nose

las orejas (una oreja) – ears (one ear)

pequeño/pequeña – little (m/f)

una boca – a mouth/one mouth

rojo/roja – red (m/f)

diez – ten

los dedos (un dedo) – fingers

largo/larga – long (m/f)

los brazos (un brazo) – arms (one arm)

los dedos del pie – toes

las piernas (una pierna) – legs (one leg)

fuerte – strong

Follow-up work

Remind the children about the agreement of nouns and adjectives to show masculine, feminine, singular and plural forms, eg

el dedo del pie pequeño (m sing)

la oreja pequeña (f sing)

los dedos del pie pequeños (m pl)

las orejas pequeñas (f pl)

Introduce the vocabulary **tiene** (he/she/it has). As a class, compose a 'Monster's body' song to sing with the backing track (track 14), eg

Tiene diez ojos verdes

Y cuatro orejas.

Tiene siete pies rosas

Y tres manos blancas, manos blancas.

In the chorus, replace **el cuerpo humano** with **el cuerpo del monstruo**.

El cuerpo

El cuerpo, el cuerpo,
Todos somos diferentes.
¡El cuerpo humano es magnífico!
¡Magnífico!

Tengo dos ojos grandes
Y una nariz.
Tengo dos orejas pequeñas
Y una boca roja, boca roja.

El cuerpo, el cuerpo ...

Tengo diez dedos largos
Y dos brazos largos.
Tengo diez dedos del pie pequeños
Y dos piernas fuertes, piernas fuertes.

El cuerpo, el cuerpo ...

De once a veinte

Using the song

Make a set of number cards from eleven to twenty using the photocopiable number cards on page 63. (To do this, make multiple copies of number 10 and layer other digits over the tens or units digits as appropriate.) Display the cards as a number track. Listen to the song (track 15) with the class and point to each number on the number line as it occurs in the song, inviting the children to join in with the second voice (female singer) on the echoes.

Teach the number sequence from eleven to twenty by listening to the song again or by saying the numbers yourself for the children to copy. Practise the numbers by singing them with track 15.

Divide into two groups to sing the whole song: each group joins in with either the male or female part during the echo sections and everyone joins together for the rest of the song. Swap parts so that each group has a turn at leading the echo sections. When the whole song is familiar, perform it in two groups with the backing track (track 16).

Developing the vocabulary

Make two sets of number cards from one to twenty. Teach the number **cero** (zero), then all sit in a circle and play ¡**Cero!** Give a number card to each child, ensuring that there are two children allocated to some of the numbers. (For smaller groups, just use the numbers one to ten or eleven to twenty.) Make sure that the children can recognise the name of their number.

Now call out numbers at random. The child with that number must stand up, then sit down when the next is called. If two children have the same number they must quickly swap places in the circle. If you call out ¡**Cero!** everyone passes their number card to the person on their left. As the children become familiar with the numbers, speed up the tempo of the game.

key vocabulary

once – eleven
doce – twelve
trece – thirteen
catorce – fourteen
quince – fifteen
dieciséis – sixteen
diecisiete – seventeen
dieciocho – eighteen
diecinueve – nineteen
veinte – twenty

Follow-up work

Play **Bingo** with the class. Each child draws a grid of twelve squares and writes in any twelve numbers between zero and twenty. Shuffle a set of number cards 0–20, then call them out one at a time.

When the children hear a number they have written down, they cross it off their grid. The first child to cross off all twelve numbers shouts **Bingo** and wins the game.

Teach the numbers from twenty-one to thirty: **veintiuno, veintidós, veintitrés, veinticuatro, veinticinco, veintiséis, veintisiete, veintiocho, veintinueve, treinta**. Play **Bingo** again, using numbers from zero to thirty.

De once a veinte

Once	once
Doce	doce
Trece	trece
Catorce	catorce

Once, doce, trece, catorce, quince.

Once, doce, trece, catorce, quince.

Dieciséis	dieciséis
Diecisiete	diecisiete
Dieciocho	dieciocho
Diecinueve	diecinueve

Dieciséis, diecisiete, dieciocho,
diecinueve, Veinte, veinte.

Once, doce, trece, catorce, quince.
Dieciséis, diecisiete, dieciocho,
diecinueve, veinte.

Vamos

Tracks   the song   backing track   spoken phrases

Using the song

Listen to the song (track 17). Introduce the phrase **¡Buena idea!** and all join in with this phrase each time it is repeated.

Teach the verses one at a time using track 46 or by saying the words yourself for the children to copy. As the children learn the meaning of each verse, encourage them to add actions representing the activities to help them memorise the words.

When the class is familiar with the whole song, sing it with track 17, then with the backing track (track 18).

Developing the vocabulary

Introduce more vocabulary for places to visit and activities, eg

a la casa (to the house/home)

a la piscina (to the swimming pool)

al mercado (to the market)

a la ciudad (to the city)

al cine (to the cinema)

ver la tele (to watch TV)

ver una película (to watch a film)

ir a comprar (to go shopping)

With the whole class, create new verses for the song and sing them with the backing track (track 18), eg

¡Vamos a la casa!
¡Buena idea! ¡Buena idea!
¡Vamos a la casa,
A ver la tele!

key vocabulary

vamos – let's go
a la playa – to the beach
¡Buena idea! – Good idea!
vamos a nadar – let's go swimming
en el mar – in the sea
a la montaña – to the mountain(s)
trepar – to climb/climbing
y – and
esquiar – to ski/skiing
a la plaza – to the town square
escuchar la música – to listen to the music
al río – to the river
pescar – to fish/fishing
caminar – to walk/walking
a la fiesta – to the fiesta (festival)
bailar – to dance/dancing
cantar – to sing/singing

Follow-up work

When the children have learnt vocabulary for days of the week and/or time, teach the question **¿Cuándo?** (When?) and possible answers, eg

por la mañana (in the morning)

por la tarde (in the afternoon)

por la noche (in the evening)

el lunes, el martes ... (on Monday, on Tuesday ...)

Also teach the phrases **de acuerdo** (OK) and **no es posible** (that's no good). Ask the children to work in small groups to practise the vocabulary they have learnt and plan a role play, eg

¡Vamos al cine!
¡Buena idea! ¿Cuándo?
El domingo, por la tarde.
Sí, sí, de acuerdo.

Vamos

¡Vamos a la playa!
¡Buena idea! ¡Buena idea!
¡Vamos a nadar,
Nadar en el mar!

¡Vamos a la montaña!
¡Buena idea! ¡Buena idea!
¡Vamos a trepar,
Trepar y esquiar!

¡Vamos a la plaza!
¡Buena idea! ¡Buena idea!
¡Vamos a escuchar,
Escuchar la música!

¡Vamos al río!
¡Buena idea! ¡Buena idea!
¡Vamos a pescar,
Pescar y caminar!

¡Vamos a la fiesta!
¡Buena idea! ¡Buena idea!
¡Vamos a bailar,
Bailar y cantar!

¡Vamos a la plaza!
¡Buena idea! ¡Buena idea!
¡Vamos a escuchar,
Escuchar la música!

¡Vamos! ¡Vamos!

photocopiable

Dad palmadas

Tracks   **19** the chant   **20** backing track

Using the song

Listen to the song (track 19), all joining in with the clapping patterns as they become familiar. Ask the children if they can guess the meaning of **¡Dad palmadas!** Listen to the song again, joining in with the phrase **¡Dad palmadas!** and clapping the rhythms.

Teach the verses one at a time, demonstrating different ways of clapping to match the meaning of the words. Ask the class to observe the different ways of clapping and to see if they can guess the meaning of the words in the song. Point out that **¡Escuchad la música!** is similar to the phrase **Escuchar la música** (which may be familiar from the song **Vamos**) but this time it is an instruction.

When everyone is confident with the vocabulary and the clapping styles and rhythms, sing the whole song with track 19 and then with the backing track (track 20).

key vocabulary

dad palmadas – clap your hands
rápidamente – quickly
lentamente – slowly
escucha/escuchad la música – listen to the music (sing/pl)
a la derecha – to the right
a la izquierda – to the left
fuerte – loudly/strongly
suave – quietly/gently
arriba – up/above
abajo – down/below
todo recto – straight ahead

Developing the vocabulary

To reinforce the vocabulary, play the game **¡Dad palmadas!** with the class. Call out **¡Dad palmadas!** using the rhythm from the song. The class responds by clapping the rhythm of the words. Then call out an instruction using the rhythm from the song, eg **a la derecha**. The children respond by clapping the rhythm in the appropriate manner: in this case, to the right of their bodies. Repeat using different phrases from the song. If you call out **¡Silencio!** everyone must keep still.

Teach the children to recognise the meaning of other instructional language you might use in the classroom, eg

Repite/Repetid (Repeat, sing/pl)   **Ven/Venid aquí** (Come here)
Mira/Mirad (Look)   **Escucha/Escuchad** (Listen)
Para/Parad (Stop)   **Enséñame/Enseñadme** (Show me)
Levántate/Levantaos (Stand up)   **Siéntate/Sentaos** (Sit down)

Play the game **¡Dad palmadas!** again, incorporating some of this language as an extension to the game. This time the children respond with appropriate actions.

Follow-up work

Set up an obstacle course in a large space, eg using bean bags or cones in the school hall or playground. Explain that the objective is to safely guide a blindfolded traveller along the route with verbal instructions, eg

Todo recto ... lentamente ... a la derecha ... todo recto ... ¡Para!

Blindfold a volunteer and demonstrate giving instructions in Spanish to safely guide them to the end of the route. Then invite confident individuals to give the instructions to guide other travellers.

Divide the class into small groups. Each group designs a new route, then individuals take it in turns to guide a blindfolded traveller along the route.

Dad palmadas

¡Dad palmadas!
¡Dad palmadas!
Rápidamente,
Lentamente.
¡Escuchad la música!

¡Dad palmadas!
¡Dad palmadas!
A la derecha,
A la izquierda.
¡Escuchad la música!

¡Dad palmadas!
¡Dad palmadas!
Fuerte, fuerte,
Suave, suave.
¡Escuchad la música!

¡Dad palmadas!
¡Dad palmadas!
Arriba, abajo,
Todo recto.
¡Escuchad la música!

¡Dad palmadas!

La semana

Tracks   **21** the song   **22** backing track

Using the song

Explain to the children that they are going to learn the names of the days of the week. All listen to the song (track 21).

Teach the vocabulary for the days of the week, either by listening to the song and joining in as they are repeated, or by saying the words yourself for the children to copy. Teach the remaining parts of the song, ensuring that the children understand the meaning of the words.

Sing the whole song several times until everyone is confident with the vocabulary, then perform it with the backing track (track 22).

Developing the vocabulary

Make an enlarged photocopy of the days of the week cards on the song sheet. Explain to the class that in Spanish the days of the week do not start with capital letters as they do in English. Display the cards and point to each in turn as you all sing the song.

Introduce the following phrases and vocabulary:

¿Qué día es hoy? (What day is it today?)

Hoy es ... (Today is ...)

¿Y ayer? (And yesterday?)

¿Y mañana? (And tomorrow?)

Make a daily habit of asking the class these three questions at registration until the children are confident at naming all the days of the week. Each day, select an individual to collect the appropriate day of the week card and display it in the classroom.

key vocabulary

la semana – the week
lunes – Monday
martes – Tuesday
miércoles – Wednesday
jueves – Thursday
viernes – Friday
sábado – Saturday
domingo – Sunday
los días (un día) – the days (a day)
siete – seven
de la semana – of the week
hoy – today
ayer – yesterday
y – and
mañana – tomorrow
repite/repetid – repeat (sing/pl)
uno – one
dos – two
tres – three
cuatro – four
cinco – five
seis – six

Follow-up work

Ask the children to design a personal diary (**un diario**) for one week, showing the days of the week in Spanish and drawing real or imaginary events for each day. Remind them to use lower case letters, eg **lunes**.

When the children have learnt vocabulary relating to the weather, ask individuals to describe the daily weather, eg

Hoy es lunes. Hace calor.

(Today is Monday. It is hot.)

Record this by drawing a weather symbol on a grid showing the names of the days of the week. Use the completed grid for group discussions, eg

El lunes hace calor. El martes llueve.

(On Monday it is hot. On Tuesday it is raining.)

La semana

Lunes, martes, miércoles,
Jueves, viernes,
Sábado, domingo.
Lunes, martes, miércoles,
Jueves, viernes,
Sábado, domingo.
La semana.

Los siete días de la semana,
Hoy, ayer, y mañana.
Los siete días de la semana,
Hoy, ayer, y mañana, mañana.

----

repetid

Uno dos tres cuatro cinco
seis siete, La semana.

lunes

martes

miércoles

jueves

viernes

sábado

domingo

photocopiable

Mi familia

introducing oneself and family members

Tracks **23** the song **24** backing track **47** spoken phrases

Using the song

Enlarge and cut out the individual pictures of the González family members on the photocopiable song sheet, and the picture of the baby on this page. Hold up the cards one by one and introduce the class to the characters' names. Keep the María card and invite five children to stand in a line facing the class, holding up the remaining cards in the following order: Lucía, Alberto, padre, madre, José.

All listen to the song (track 23). Point to each card in turn during the chorus, as the words **Mi hermana**, **mi hermano**, **mi padre**, **mi madre y el bebé** are sung. During the first verse point to your own card, then to each of the siblings as they are named.

Teach the vocabulary of the chorus using track 47. All join in each time it is repeated. Then learn the verses line by line and practise them until the children are confident. Sing the whole song the backing track (track 24).

Alberto

photocopiable

Developing the vocabulary

Once the class is familiar with the song, choose six new individuals to play the roles of the González family. Assign a role to each child and ask the children playing the mother and father to think of Spanish names for themselves, eg Silvia and Miguel. Building on phrases from the song, the child playing the role of María introduces herself and her family to the class, eg **Yo me llamo María. Mi madre se llama Silvia. Mi hermano se llama Alberto**. Invite each of the family members in turn to introduce each other (even the baby!).

Teach the children the names for other family members, eg

el abuelo (the grandfather)   **la abuela** (the grandmother)
el tío (the uncle)   **la tía** (the aunt)
el primo/la prima (the cousin, m/f)

Introduce vocabulary to enable the children to describe their own nationality, eg

(Yo) soy inglés/inglesa (I am English, m/f)
(Yo) soy escocés/escocesa (I am Scottish, m/f)
(Yo) soy galés/galesa (I am Welsh, m/f)
(Yo) soy irlandés/irlandesa (I am Irish, m/f)

key vocabulary

mi – my
la familia – the family
ésta es – this is
la familia González – the González family
la hermana – the sister
el hermano – the brother
el padre – the father
la madre – the mother
y – and
el bebé – the baby
(yo) me llamo – my name is
(él/ella) se llama – his/her name is
(yo) soy español/española – I am Spanish (m/f)
vivo – I live
en España – in Spain
la ciudad – the city
es – is
la capital – the capital
en Madrid – in Madrid

Follow-up work

Ask the children to bring in photos or to draw portraits of people in their family. Revise **(yo) tengo** (I have) and introduce the additional vocabulary:

(él/ella) tiene (he/she has)
(ellos/ellas) tienen (they have, m/f)
(ellos/ellas) se llaman (they are called, m/f)

Encourage the children to use this with vocabulary already learnt to describe themselves and members of their family. Each child could prepare a presentation for the class, eg

¡Hola! Me llamo Max. Soy galés. Tengo once años. Tengo dos hermanas. Ellas se llaman Bethan y Rachel. Ellas tienen trece años y quince años.

Mi familia

Ésta es mi familia,
La familia González.
Mi hermana, mi hermano,
Mi padre, mi madre y el bebé.

Yo me llamo María,
Mi hermana se llama Lucía,
Mi hermano se llama Alberto Y
el bebé se llama José.
Yo soy española,
Vivo en España.
Mi ciudad es la capital,
Vivo en Madrid.

Ésta es mi familia ...

Yo me llamo Alberto,
Mi hermana se llama Lucía,
Mi hermana se llama María
Y el bebé se llama José.
Yo soy español,
Vivo en España.
Mi ciudad es la capital,
Vivo en Madrid.

Ésta es mi familia ...

madre

padre

María

Alberto

Lucía

Feliz cumpleaños

months of the year/celebrating special occasions

Using the song

Listen to the song (track 25) and all learn to say the names of the months. Listen again and all join in with naming the months in the chanted section.

Teach the remaining vocabulary either by listening to the song or by saying the words yourself for the children to copy. Gradually learn the whole song to sing with track 25. When the children are confident, sing it with the backing track (track 26).

Developing the vocabulary

All sing the song with track 25. As the names of the months are chanted the children quickly stand up when they hear the month of their birthday and sit down again as the next is spoken.

Show the class the photocopiable song sheet and point out that capital letters are not used for the names of months in Spanish.

Teach the phrase **Mi cumpleaños es en** … (My birthday is in …). In small groups the children take it in turns to tell the rest of the group in which month is their birthday, eg

Mi cumpleaños es en octubre.

Then revise numbers one to thirty and introduce the number thirty-one: **treinta y uno**. Explain to the children how to say the date of their birthday, eg

Mi cumpleaños es el veinte de marzo.

Encourage them to respond in this way to the question **¿Cuándo es tu cumpleaños?**

Introduce more vocabulary relating to special events and festivals,

eg **una fiesta/fiesta nacional** (a holiday/bank holiday)

Navidad (Christmas)

Día de la Hispanidad (12 October, national heritage day)

Semana Santa (holy week: the week before Easter)

Carnaval (the week before Ash Wednesday)

Ask the children to use books or the internet to discover more about how these festivals are celebrated in Spanish culture.

key vocabulary

¡Feliz cumpleaños! – Happy birthday!

un cumpleaños – a birthday

hoy es mi cumpleaños – today is my birthday

la primavera – spring

el verano – summer

los doce meses del año – the twelve months of the year

en – in

el otoño – autumn

el invierno – winter

¿Cuándo es tu cumpleaños? – When is your birthday?

enero – January

febrero – February

marzo – March

abril – April

mayo – May

junio – June

julio – July

agosto – August

septiembre – September

octubre – October

noviembre – November

diciembre – December

Follow-up work

Divide the class into groups and give one group a calendar which has the twelve months of the year in Spanish. Each child takes it in turn to ask another group member when his or her birthday is, eg

David, ¿cuándo es tu cumpleaños?

David answers, eg **Mi cumpleaños es en julio**, and the questioner writes his name in the correct place on the calendar.

When the birthdays of everyone in the group have been recorded, it is passed on to the other groups in turn. The completed calendar of class birthdays can be displayed in the classroom and used throughout the year to reinforce the vocabulary.

Describe the Spanish tradition of **tirar de las orejas**, in which a child whose birthday it is has their ear pulled (by the earlobe) as many times as the number of years he or she is celebrating.

Feliz cumpleaños

¡Feliz cumpleaños!
¡Cumpleaños!
¡Cumpleaños feliz!
Hoy es mi cumpleaños.
¡Cumpleaños!
¡Cumpleaños feliz!

La primavera, el verano,
Los doce meses del año.
¿En el otoño, el invierno,
Cuándo es tu cumpleaños?

enero	febrero
marzo	abril
mayo	junio
julio	agosto
septiembre	octubre
noviembre	diciembre

¡Feliz cumpleaños! ...

la primavera

el verano

el otoño

el invierno

photocopiable

¿Adónde vas?

asking questions and making statements about travel

Using the song

All listen to the song (track 27), joining in with the chorus as it becomes familiar. Teach the children the meaning of the words of the chorus.

Ask the class to listen to the verses to see if they can recognise any vocabulary or guess its meaning, eg **Barcelona**, **autobús**, **bicicleta**. Teach the verses one at a time, then sing the whole song with track 27.

When the children are confident, sing the song with the backing track (track 28). You may wish to allocate each verse to a different individual or small group. Everyone joins together to sing the chorus.

Developing the vocabulary

Introduce vocabulary for other forms of transport, eg

en coche (by car)

en tren (by train)

en barco (by boat)

en metro (by underground)

en avión (by plane)

In groups, the children create a new verse for the song, using vocabulary they already know and a means of transport, eg

Yo voy a la playa,
Yo voy en coche ...

Sing the new verses with the backing track (track 28).

You may wish to introduce the children to more forms of the verb **ir** (to go):

(tú) vas (you go, sing informal)

(él/ella) va (he/she goes)

(nosotros/nosotras) vamos (we go, m/f)

(vosotros/vosotras) vais (you go, pl informal, m/f)

(ellos/ellas) van (they go, m/f)

key vocabulary

¿Adónde vas? – Where are you going?

mi – my

un amigo/una amiga – a friend (m/f)

¿A un buen lugar? – Somewhere good?

(yo) voy – I go/I am going

a Barcelona – to Barcelona

en autobús – by bus

sí – yes

a la piscina – to the swimming pool

en bicicleta/en bici – by bicycle

a tu casa – to your house

a pie – on foot

Follow-up work

Carry out a class survey of the means of transport used to travel to school. Ask individuals around the class **¿Cómo vas al colegio?** (How do you go to school?).

They reply giving the means of transport they use, eg

(Yo) voy al colegio en tren y a pie.
(I go to school by train and on foot.)

As a class, draw a bar chart to show the number of children who use each means of transport. Encourage the children to discuss the totals, eg

Nueve alumnos van al colegio en coche. (Nine pupils go to school by car.)

Ask the children to list the names of some Spanish towns. They can then practise travel vocabulary by discussing imaginary holiday journeys.

¿Adónde vas?

¿Adónde vas? ¿Adónde vas?
¿Adónde vas, mi amiga?
¿Adónde vas? ¿Adónde vas?
¿Adónde vas? ¿A un buen lugar?

Yo voy a Barcelona,
Yo voy en autobús.
¡Sí, sí, sí! Voy en autobús.

¿Adónde vas? ¿Adónde vas?
¿Adónde vas, mi amigo?
¿Adónde vas? ¿Adónde vas?
¿Adónde vas? ¿A un buen lugar?

Yo voy a la piscina,
Yo voy en bicicleta.
¡Sí, sí, sí! Voy en bicicleta.

¿Adónde vas? ¿Adónde vas?
¿Adónde vas, mi amiga?
¿Adónde vas? ¿Adónde vas?
¿Adónde vas? ¿A un buen lugar?

Yo voy a tu casa,
Yo voy, sí, voy a pie.
¡Sí, sí, sí! Voy, voy, voy a pie.

¿Adónde vas? ¿Adónde vas?
¿Adónde vas, mi amigo?
¿Adónde vas? ¿Adónde vas?
¿Adónde vas? ¿A un buen lugar?

photocopiable

Tapas, patatas

expressing likes and dislikes/ordering food and drinks

Using the song

Explain to the children that they are going to learn vocabulary related to eating and drinking. Play track 29 and ask them to identify any words they recognise or can guess the meaning of, eg **patatas**, **cola**, **limonada**, **café**, **chocolate**.

Teach the song line by line, either by listening to track 48 or by saying the words yourself for the children to copy. You could ask individuals to hold up pictures of the food and drink at the front of the class as a reminder of the sequence in each verse.

When the class is familiar with the vocabulary, sing the whole song with the backing track (track 30). Confident individuals or pairs of children may sing lines of the song in response to the whole class singing the questions together.

Developing the vocabulary

Extend the children's vocabulary by introducing the following phrases:

tengo hambre (I'm hungry)

tengo sed (I'm thirsty)

el menú del día (the menu/dish of the day)

¿Está bueno? (Is it good?)

Está rico/muy rico (It's delicious)

No está mal (It's not bad)

La cuenta, por favor (The bill, please)

Show the children labelled illustrations of food and drink to extend their vocabulary, eg

los churros (doughnuts/fritters)

el té (tea)

un pastel (a cake)

un bocadillo de jamón/queso (a ham/cheese sandwich)

el pescado (fish)

el pollo (chicken)

la leche (milk)

As a class, compose new verses to sing with the backing track (track 30).

key vocabulary

las tapas – appetisers

las patatas (una patata) – potatoes (a potato)

el gazpacho – gazpacho (tomato soup, served cold)

la paella – paella

el pan – bread

¿Qué quieres comer? – What would you like to eat?

un helado – an ice cream

por favor – please

¿Qué quieres beber? – What would you like to drink?

(yo) quiero – I would like

la cola (una cola) – cola (a cola)

me gusta – I like

el pan tostado – toast

¡Es delicioso/deliciosa! – It's delicious! (m/f)

la limonada – lemonade

no me gusta – I don't like

el café – coffee

una tortilla – an omelette

el zumo (un zumo) – juice (a juice)

la ensalada – salad

el agua fría – cold water

el chocolate (un chocolate) – chocolate (a hot chocolate)

Follow-up work

Discuss with the children cultural traditions relating to food in Spain, such as **tapas** – small dishes served on their own or before a main meal.

Ask the children to research recipes for Spanish food using books or the internet. If possible, let them make and taste a Spanish omelette (**una tortilla**) or other typical foods.

Set up a café (**un café**) in the classroom with tables and chairs. The children can design menus using food and drink vocabulary they have learnt. In small groups, they take it in turns to play the role of waiter/waitress (**el camarero/la camarera**) and customers. Each waiter/waitress invites individuals to order food and drinks from the menus.

Tapas, patatas

Tapas, patatas, gazpacho, paella,
Tapas, patatas, gazpacho, pan.
Tapas, patatas, gazpacho, paella,
Tapas, patatas, pan.

'¿Qué quieres comer?'
'Un helado, por favor.'
'¿Qué quieres beber?'
'Quiero una cola, por favor.'
Me gusta el pan tostado.
¡Es delicioso!
Me gusta la limonada.
No me gusta el café.

Tapas, patatas, gazpacho, paella …

'¿Qué quieres comer?'
'Una tortilla, por favor.'
'¿Qué quieres beber?'
'Quiero un zumo, por favor.'
Me gusta la ensalada.
¡Es deliciosa!
Me gusta el agua fría.
¡No me gusta el chocolate!

SINGING SPANISH © HELEN MACGREGOR & STEPHEN CHADWICK 2008, HarperCollins*Publishers* Ltd

La Bella Durmiente

Tracks **31** the song **32** backing track **49** spoken phrases

Using the song

Remind the children of the main outline of the story of Sleeping Beauty to ensure that they are all familiar with the story. Listen to the song (track 31) and add appropriate actions to convey the events described in the song. Encourage the children to join in with the actions.

Teach the numbers in the chanted sections of the song. Make a set of cards showing multiples of ten up to one hundred and display these in a line where the class can see. Point to the numbers as you say them or listen to them in the song. When the children are confident, all join in with the chanted numbers in the song.

Teach the verses one at a time, either by listening to track 49 or by saying the words yourself for the class to copy. Perform actions and use the repeating phrases in the song for practice.

Finally, perform the whole song with track 31, then with the backing track (track 32). Three children may like to mime the parts of the princess, the witch and the prince as you sing.

Developing the vocabulary

Revise the numbers from one to ten and discuss with the class similarities between these words and the words for multiples of ten up to one hundred. All say the word **cien** out loud. Ask the children if they can think of any words in English which begin in a similar way, eg century, centimetre, centurion, centilitre.

Practise the number vocabulary by inviting ten children to the front of the class and giving them cards showing multiples of ten up to one hundred. Point to each number and say it for the class to copy. Then choose numbers in a random order, signalling which child should hold up their card with a tap on the shoulder. The rest of the class calls out the number.

Teach the children how to say other numbers, eg

treinta y uno (31)   **setenta y uno (71)**
treinta y dos (32)   **setenta y dos (72)**
treinta y tres (33)   **setenta y tres (73)**

key vocabulary

la Bella Durmiente – Sleeping Beauty
había una vez – once upon a time there was
una princesa – a princess
(él/ella) vino – he/she came
una bruja – a witch
muy – very
malo/mala – bad/wicked (m/f)
la princesa se pinchó un dedo – the princess pricked her finger
(él/ella) durmió – he/she slept
repite/repetid – repeat (sing/pl)
diez – ten
veinte – twenty
treinta – thirty
cuarenta – forty
cincuenta – fifty
sesenta – sixty
setenta – seventy
ochenta – eighty
noventa – ninety
cien – one hundred
(los) años – years
un bosque creció – a forest grew
alrededor – around
un príncipe – a prince
guapo – handsome
cortó – he cut
las ramas – the branches
con – with
su espada – his sword
despertó a la bella – he woke the beautiful girl
un beso (los besos) – a kiss (kisses)

Follow-up work

Revise the numbers already learnt and play **OXO** with the class. Each child draws a three by three grid and writes in nine different numbers (using numbers from zero to twenty, and multiples of ten to one hundred). Place a set of number cards showing these numbers in a bag and mix them round.

Select a number and call out its name. Any child with this number repeats the name and then draws an O on the number if it is in an outside square, or an X if it is in the central square.

Continue drawing numbers from the bag. The first child to complete a line of three numbers through the centre of their grid shouts **OXO** and wins the game. The winner may like to call out the numbers when you play the game again.

La Bella Durmiente

Había una vez, había una vez,
Había una vez una princesa.
Vino una bruja, vino una bruja,
Vino una bruja, muy mala.

La princesa se pinchó, se pinchó un dedo, Se pinchó un dedo, la princesa durmió. [repetid]
Diez, veinte, treinta, cuarenta,
Cincuenta, sesenta, setenta,
ochenta, Noventa, cien años.

Un bosque creció, un bosque creció,
Un bosque creció alrededor.
Vino un príncipe, vino un príncipe,
Vino un príncipe, muy guapo.

Cortó las ramas, las ramas, las ramas, Cortó las ramas con su espada. [repetid]
Diez, veinte, treinta, cuarenta,
Cincuenta, sesenta, setenta,
ochenta, Noventa, cien ramas.

Despertó a la bella, despertó a la bella, Despertó a la bella con un beso.
Diez, veinte, treinta, cuarenta,
Cincuenta, sesenta, setenta,
ochenta, Noventa, cien besos.
¡Cien besos!
¡Cien besos!

Mi paga

buying things/simple prices/expressing likes and dislikes

Tracks — **33** the song — **34** backing track — **50** spoken phrases

Using the song

Explain to the class that they are going to learn a song about going shopping to spend pocket money. All listen to the song (track 33). Ask the children if they can recognise or guess any of the items that were bought. (A football, a CD and a games console.) Did they recognise any other phrases or words during the conversation verses, eg **tengo**, **por favor**, **gracias**, **ocho euros**, **fantástico**?

Listen to track 33 again, all joining in with the chorus as it becomes familiar. Ensure the children understand the meaning of the vocabulary.

Teach the verses one at a time, either using track 50 or by saying the words yourself for the children to copy. When the children are confident, sing the whole song with track 33 then with the backing track (track 34), dividing into two groups to perform the conversations if you wish.

Developing the vocabulary

Draw attention to the phrases from the song: **¿Te gusta éste?** and **¿Te gusta ésta?** Explain that they agree with the masculine or feminine nouns to which they refer, ie

¿Te gusta éste? refers to **un balón** or **un CD**;

¿Te gusta ésta? refers to **una consola**.

Introduce more vocabulary for items the children might buy with their pocket money and phrases for expressing likes and dislikes, eg

un peluche (a soft toy)

un juego (a game)

unos caramelos (some sweets)

¡Es una porquería! (It's rubbish!)

¡Ñam, ñam!/¡Riquísimo! (Yum!)

¡Qué asco!/¡Puaj! (Yuck!)

me encanta (I love)

no me gusta nada (I hate)

key vocabulary

mi – my
la paga – the pocket money
tengo – I have/I've got
voy de compras – I'm going to buy/I'm going shopping
un balón – a football
un CD – a CD
o – or
una consola – a games console
¿Qué quieres? – What would you like?
por favor – please
¿Cuánto es? – How much is it?
son – it is
ocho – eight
los euros (un euro) – euros (one euro)
¿Te gusta éste/ésta? – Do you like this one? (m/f)
sí – yes
es chulo – it's cool
aquí tienes – here you are
gracias – thank you
quince – fifteen
es fantástico – it's fantastic
noventa – ninety
es genial – it's brilliant

Follow-up work

Set up a market or supermarket (**un mercado /un supermercado**) in the classroom using items and foods whose names are familiar. Ask the children to make price labels for the items in euros using numbers they have learnt. In pairs, the children practise role-playing the shopkeeper and customer, using vocabulary from the song in their conversations.

The children can also use pictures or props from the shop to practise vocabulary expressing likes and dislikes, eg

Me encanta la leche. (I love milk.)

No me gusta nada el pescado.

(I hate fish.)

Mi paga

Tengo mi paga. Voy de compras
Un balón, un CD o una consola.
Tengo, tengo mi paga.

'¿Qué quieres?'
'Un balón, por favor. ¿Cuánto es?'
'Son ocho euros. ¿Te gusta éste?'
'Sí, es chulo.'
'Aquí tienes.'
'Gracias.'

Tengo mi paga. Voy de compras ...

'¿Qué quieres?'
'Un CD, por favor. ¿Cuánto es?'
'Son quince euros. ¿Te gusta éste?'
'Sí, es fantástico.'
'Aquí tienes.'
'Gracias.'

Tengo mi paga. Voy de compras ...

'¿Qué quieres?'
'Una consola, por favor. ¿Cuánto es?'
'Son noventa euros. ¿Te gusta ésta?'
'Sí, es genial.'
'Aquí tienes.'
'Gracias.'

¿Te gusta ésta?

Tengo mi paga. Voy de compras ...

photocopiable

¿Qué tiempo hace?

describing the weather

Tracks   **35** the song   **36** backing track   **51** spoken phrases

Using the song

All listen to the song (track 35) and ask the class to guess what the song is about. Listen again, all joining in with the first two and last two lines of the chorus. Display a map of Spain and point to the north, south, east and west on the map during the line **Norte, sur, este, oeste**. Then learn the rest of the chorus, ensuring that the children understand the meaning of the words.

Enlarge and cut out the weather symbols on the song sheet. Teach the song line by line either by listening to track 51 or by saying the words yourself for the class to copy. Fix the appropriate weather symbols to the map in the north, south, east and west of the country to reinforce the meaning of the lyrics.

When the children are familiar with the whole song, sing it first with track 35 and then with the backing track (track 36).

Developing the vocabulary

Introduce more vocabulary connected with the weather, eg

hace fresco (it is chilly)

hay niebla (it is foggy)

hay tormenta (it is stormy)

un arco iris (a rainbow)

Use the weather symbols from the song sheet to practise weather vocabulary orally. Hold up a card and ask **¿Qué tiempo hace?** to elicit a response from the class.

When the children are confident with naming the weather symbols, stage a weather forecast. Display a large map of Spain and identify the main cities. Invite children in turn to select a card and fix it to the map, using vocabulary they have learnt to describe the weather, eg

En Sevilla hace sol.

En el este llueve.

Use the completed map to question the class orally, eg

¿Dónde nieva? (Where is it snowing?).

key vocabulary

¿Qué tiempo hace? – What's the weather like?

hoy – today

(hace) mal tiempo – (it is) bad weather

(hace) buen tiempo – (it is) good weather

hace sol – it is sunny

llueve – it is raining

nieva – it is snowing

en el norte – in the north

en el sur – in the south

en el este – in the east

en el oeste – in the west

hace frío – it is cold

hace viento – it is windy

hace calor – it is hot

Es el pronóstico del tiempo para España – This is the weather forecast for Spain

Follow-up work

Practise weather vocabulary daily, asking the class questions and incorporating vocabulary already learnt, eg

Hoy es lunes. ¿Qué tiempo hace hoy? (It's Monday. What's the weather like today?)

If possible show the class a Spanish weather forecast on television. Ask the children if they recognise any words or phrases.

Ask the class to research typical climates for the Spanish Mediterranean coast, the Atlantic coast and the centre of the country, using books or the internet. Compare these with British temperatures. Talk about how the warm climate in many parts of Spain affects daily routine and shop opening hours.

¿Qué tiempo hace?

¿Qué tiempo hace hoy,
Hace hoy, hoy, hoy?
¿Mal tiempo, buen tiempo,
Hace sol, llueve, nieva?
Norte, sur, este, oeste.
¿Qué tiempo hace hoy,
Hace hoy, hoy, hoy?

♪ Es el pronóstico del tiempo para España ...

En el norte hace frío,
Frío, frío, frío.

En el sur hace sol,
Sol, sol, sol.

En el este hace viento,
Viento, viento, viento.

En el oeste hace calor,
Calor, calor, calor.

¿Qué tiempo hace hoy ...

  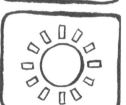 

El abecedario

Using the song

Show the class an enlarged photocopy of the alphabet on the photocopiable song sheet.

Listen to the song (track 37), pointing to each letter in turn during the alphabet section to familiarise the class with the letter names. Join in with the chorus as it becomes familiar and encourage the children to guess the meaning of the words of the chorus. Ask them if they can think why 'alphabet' in Spanish is **el abecedario**. (It is a word made up of the Spanish names of the first letters of the alphabet.)

All practise the pronunciation of individual letter names, either using the song or by saying the letter names yourself for the children to copy. Repeat until everyone is confident, then ask a child to conduct by pointing to the letters in turn as the class performs to the backing track (track 38).

Developing the vocabulary

Play **¿Cómo se escribe?** (How do you spell it?). Display an alphabet chart or an enlarged copy of the song sheet where everyone can see. Select a simple word from vocabulary already learnt, eg **Hola**.

Invite an individual to point to the matching letters on the chart as you call out the letter names one at a time for the class to repeat. When the word has been identified, write it on the board or on a display card to place on the classroom wall.

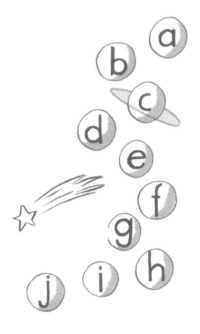

key vocabulary

el abecedario – the alphabet

a, be, ce, de, e, efe, ge, hache, i, jota, ka, ele, eme, ene, eñe, o, pe, cu, erre, ese, te, u, uve, uve doble, equis, i griega, zeta – A, B, C etc

las letras – the letters

del abecedario – of the alphabet

fantástico – fantastic

Follow-up work

Revise the following phrases:

¿Cómo te llamas?
(Yo) me llamo ...
¿Cómo se escribe?

Give the children the opportunity to spell their own names in Spanish. Some may be able to spell both first name and surname.

As a class, play **¿Quién es?** (Who is it?). Secretly select an individual in the class. Spell out in Spanish the letters of their first name, for the class to identify who it is. Repeat with other children's names. Confident children may like to lead the game.

For more of a challenge, mix up the letters of a child's name, saying them out loud as an anagram. Ask the children to write down each letter, then re-order them to work out the name.

El abecedario

Las letras, las letras, las letras, las letras,
Las letras, las letras del abecedario.
Las letras, las letras, las letras, las letras,
Las letras, las letras. ¡Fantástico!

A B C D E F G (E F G)
H I J K L M N (M N)
Ñ O P Q R S T (S T)
U V W X Y Z (Z)

Las letras, las letras,
las letras, las letras,
Las letras, las letras del abecedario.
Las letras, las letras, las letras,
las letras,
Las letras, las letras. ¡Fantástico!

El mundo es un pañuelo

names of countries/asking where someone is from

Using the song

Listen to the song (track 39), then teach the class the chorus (**Mira el mapa del mundo ...**) using the song or by saying the words yourself for the class to copy. Explain the meaning of the words of the chorus and the phrase **el mundo es un pañuelo**.

Listen to the song again and ask the children if they can identify the countries named in the song. Teach the names of the countries, then practise the alliterative responses by calling out the countries one by one for the class to give the appropriate reply.

When everyone is familiar with the vocabulary, perform the song together, first with track 39 and then with the backing track (track 40). Sing the chorus together and divide into two groups to perform the names of the countries and the responses. Swap over so that everyone has a chance to sing both parts.

Developing the vocabulary

Make a set of six cards showing the names of the countries from the middle section of the song. Shuffle the cards and place them face down. Invite six children each to select a card, keeping it hidden from the rest of the class. They stand in line and call out in turn the name of the country on their card. The class replies with the alliterative response.

Introduce the class to names of other countries, eg

Inglaterra (England)

Escocia (Scotland)

Gales (Wales)

Irlanda (Ireland)

Estados Unidos (United States)

In pairs, play **¿De dónde eres?** Each child chooses a country. Using vocabulary they have already learnt the pair enacts a role play, eg

Buenos días. ¿Cómo te llamas?   **Me llamo Alicia.**

¿De dónde eres?   **De México. ¿Y tú?**

Soy de Brasil.

key vocabulary

el mundo es un pañuelo – it's a small world (literally 'the world is a handkerchief')

mira/mirad – look at (sing/pl)

el mapa del mundo – the map of the world

¿De dónde eres? – Where do you come from?

de – from

Gran Bretaña – Great Britain

Francia – France

fantástico – fantastic

Brasil – Brazil

muy bien – very good

México – Mexico

magnífico – magnificent

Bélgica – Belgium

bellísimo – very beautiful

España – Spain

excelente – excellent

Chile – Chile

chulísimo – very cool

Follow-up work

Show the class a large map of the world. Remind the children of the countries they have learnt and locate them on the map. Introduce the vocabulary **Sudamérica** (South America), **Centroamérica** (Central America) and **Norteamérica** (North America).

Ask the class to research using books or the internet to find some of the Spanish-speaking countries of the world, eg in South and Central America. Encourage the children to learn the names of the countries and to mark them on the map, eg by making national flags attached to pins.

El mundo es un pañuelo

Mira el mapa del mundo,
Mira el mapa del mundo.
¿De dónde eres? De Gran Bretaña.
¡El mundo es un pañuelo!

De Francia   ¡Fantástico!
De Brasil   ¡Muy bien!
De México   ¡Magnífico!
¡El mundo es un pañuelo!

De Bélgica   ¡Bellísimo!
De España   ¡Excelente!
De Chile   ¡Chulísimo!
¡El mundo es un pañuelo!

Mira el mapa del mundo ...

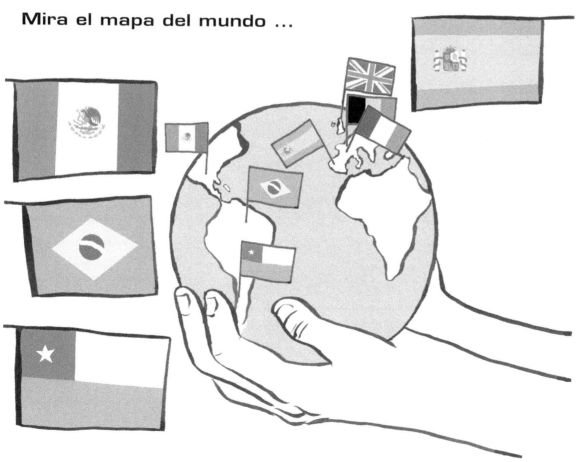

¿Qué hora es?

telling the time on the hour/names of school subjects

Tracks **41** the song **42** backing track

Using the song

All listen to the song (track 41), joining in with the **tic-tac** lines each time they occur. Gradually learn the chorus and ask the class to translate the times by recalling number vocabulary they have learnt. All sing the chorus with track 41.

Teach the verses line by line. Draw attention to the timings of the long morning session at school, with a mid-morning snack break, followed by the late lunchtime common to Spanish culture.

When everyone is familiar with the vocabulary, sing the whole song with the backing track (track 42).

Developing the vocabulary

Introduce the phrase **¿A qué hora es ...?** (What time is ...?). Ask the class questions about the timetable described in the song, eg

¿A qué hora es el inglés?

Extend the vocabulary of school subjects, eg

la historia (history)
la geografía (geography)
las ciencias (science)
la educación física (PE)
la música (music)

Use a clock face to gradually introduce more time vocabulary, eg

las ocho y media (half past eight)
la una y cuarto (quarter past one)
las once menos cuarto (quarter to eleven)

Also teach vocabulary for daily activities, eg

(yo) me levanto (I get up)
(yo) me lavo (I wash)
(yo) desayuno (I eat breakfast)
(yo) me duermo (I go to sleep)

key vocabulary

¿Qué hora es? – What's the time?

por favor – please

la una, las dos, las tres ... – one o'clock, two o'clock, three o'clock ...

a las ocho – at eight o'clock

voy al cole/al colegio – I go to school

a las nueve – at nine o'clock

tengo – I have

(las) matemáticas – maths

a las diez – at ten o'clock

(el) español – Spanish

a las once – at eleven o'clock

como – I eat

un yogur – a yogurt

tic-tac – tick tock

a las doce – at twelve o'clock

(el) inglés – English

a la una – at one o'clock

(la) informática – ICT

a las dos – at two o'clock

voy a mi casa – I go home

a las tres – at three o'clock

mi – my

la comida – lunch

Follow-up work

Ask the children to draw a cartoon strip of a real or imaginary day in their life, using vocabulary already learnt and accompanying their drawings with pictures of clocks showing the time.

Introduce the question **¿Qué haces por la mañana/la tarde/la noche?** (What do you do in the morning/afternoon/at night?).

Divide the class into small groups to have conversations about their daily life. Encourage them to ask and answer questions about each other's cartoon strips, eg

¿Qué haces por la mañana?
Yo me levanto a las siete y media.
Voy a la piscina.

¿Qué hora es?

¿Qué hora es, por favor?
¿Qué hora es, por favor?
La una, las dos, las tres,
Las cuatro, las cinco, las seis,
Las siete, las ocho, las nueve,
Las diez, las once, las doce.
¿Qué hora es?

A las ocho voy al cole,
A las nueve tengo matemáticas,
A las diez tengo español,
A las once como un yogur.
Tic-tac, tic-tac, tic-tac, tic-tac,
Tic-tac, tic-tac.

¿Qué hora es, por favor? ...

A las doce tengo inglés,
A la una tengo informática,
A las dos voy a mi casa,
A las tres como mi comida.
Tic-tac, tic-tac, tic-tac, tic-tac,
Tic-tac, tic-tac.

Tic-tac, tic-tac.
¿Qué hora es?

La ropa

Tracks
43 the song **44** backing track **52** spoken phrases

Using the song

All listen to the song (track 43) and join in with each time it is sung. Listen to the song again and teach the chorus using track 52 or by saying the words yourself for the children to copy. Finally, teach the verses which describe the items of clothing, one line at a time.

When the class is familiar with the whole song, perform it with the backing track (track 44). The children may wish to devise a dance to perform during the chorus.

Developing the vocabulary

Introduce the class to more vocabulary for items of clothing, eg

una bufanda (a scarf)

unos zapatos (some shoes)

unas botas (some boots)

un vestido (a dress)

un jersey (a jumper)

Explain the use of **unos/unas** (some, m/f), pointing out that **unos** is used with a masculine noun and **unas** with a feminine noun.

Play **Cesta de la ropa** (Laundry basket). Place colourful, fun items of clothing in two large laundry baskets, making sure each basket contains the same types of clothing. Divide the class into two teams and ask them to form a line by each basket.

Call out the name of an item of clothing, making a note of the order in which you call them out. The first child from each team quickly searches for the named item and puts it on, moving to the back of the line. Continue until all the clothing has been removed from the baskets. Then check each team's clothing against your list, naming each item aloud. The winning team is the one with the most clothes in the correct order.

Revise agreement of adjectives and practise describing items of clothing, eg **una bufanda larga**, **unos zapatos grandes**, **unas botas rojas**. Point out that many adjectives do not change to match masculine/feminine nouns, eg **grande**, **azul**, **verde**, **rosa**, **violeta**, **naranja**, **marrón**. To agree with plural nouns, add an 's' if the adjective ends in a vowel, or add 'es' if it ends in a consonant.

key vocabulary

la ropa – (the) clothes

dando vueltas – going round

baila – (it) dances

en la lavadora – in the washing machine

¡Olé! – exclamation, eg Bravo!

la camiseta – the T-shirt

la falda – the skirt

corto/corta – short (m/f)

la gorra – the cap

rojo/roja – red (m/f)

el sombrero – the sunhat

la blusa – the blouse

rosa – pink

los pantalones (un pantalón/ unos pantalones) – the trousers (a pair of trousers)

los calcetines (un calcetín) – the socks (a sock)

los vaqueros – the jeans

Follow-up work

Teach the children the phrases:

¿Qué llevas puesto hoy? (What are you wearing today?)

(Yo) llevo ... (I am wearing ...)

¿Qué lleva puesto? (What is he/she wearing?)

(Él/ella) lleva ... (He/she is wearing ...)

Using clothing from the laundry basket game, invite volunteers to dress up and present a fashion show to the class. Ask the models what they are wearing, or select presenters to describe what is being worn, eg

Nathan lleva unos vaqueros negros, una camiseta grande y unos zapatos blancos.

La ropa

Dando vueltas, dando vueltas,
Baila la ropa en la lavadora.
Dando vueltas, dando vueltas.
¡La ropa! ¡La ropa!
¡Olé, olé, olé, olé, olé!

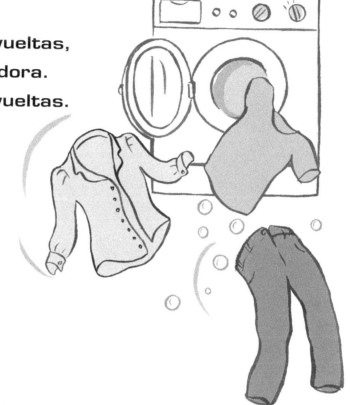

La camiseta,
La falda corta,
La gorra roja,
El sombrero.
¡La ropa! ¡La ropa!
¡Olé, olé, olé, olé, olé!

Dando vueltas, dando vueltas ...

La blusa rosa,
Los pantalones,
Los calcetines,
Los vaqueros.
¡La ropa! ¡La ropa!
¡Olé, olé, olé, olé, olé!

Dando vueltas, dando vueltas ...

¡Olé!

photocopiable

Melody lines

1 Hola (p6)

3 Buenos días (p8)

5 ¿Cuántos animales? (p10)

¿Cuán-tos a-ni-ma-les? U-no, dos, tres, Ten-go tres tor-tu-gas, U-no, dos, tres.

[4]

¿Cuán-tos a-ni-ma-les? U-no, dos, tres, Ten-go tres per-ros, U-no, dos, tres.

7 De uno a diez (p12)

U-no dos tres, U-no dos tres, Cua-tro cin-co seis, Cua-tro cin-co seis.

5

Sie-te o-cho nue-ve, Sie-te o-cho nue-ve, Diez.

9 Campeones (p14)

Quickly

¡Muy bien, muy bien, e-res un cam-pe-ón!___ ¡Muy bien, muy bien,

6

e-res u-na cam-pe-o-na! ¡Es-tu-pen-do, soy un cam-pe-ón!___ ¡Es-tu-

11   rit.   4th time FINE Slower

-pen-do, soy u-na cam-pe-o-na!   ¿Sa-bes na-dar?

                                        v. 3 ¿Sa-bes ju-gar,

16

¿Na-das bien?   Yo sé na-dar,   na-do bien.
ju-gar al fút-bol?   Yo sé ju-gar,   jue-go bien.

Melody lines

11 Mi color favorito (p16)

Mi co-lor fa-vo-ri-to es el ro-sa, ro-sa, Y me gus-ta el a-zul.

Mi co-lor fa-vo-ri-to es el a-zul, a-zul, Y me gus-ta el blan-co.

Ro-sa, ro-sa, ro-sa, A-zul, a-zul, a-zul, Blan-co, blan-co, blan-co, Ro-jo, ro-jo, ro-jo, ver-de, ma-rrón.

Mi co-lor fa-vo-ri-to es el ver-de, ver-de, No me gus-ta el ma-rrón.

13 El cuerpo (p18)

El cuer-po, el cuer-po, To-dos so-mos di-fe-ren-tes. ¡El

cuer-po hu-ma-no es mag-ní-fi-co! ¡Mag-ní-fi-co!

1. Ten-go dos o-jos gran-des Y'u-na na-riz. Ten-go dos o-re-jas pe-que-ñas Y'u-na bo-ca ro-ja, bo-ca ro-ja. El

2. Ten-go diez de-dos lar-gos Y dos bra-zos lar-gos. Ten-go diez de-dos del pie pe-que-ños Y dos pier-nas fuer-tes, pier-nas fuer-tes. El

15 De once a veinte (p20)

17 Vamos (p22)

Melody lines

19 Dad palmadas (p24)

21 La semana (p26)

23 Mi familia (p28)

25 Feliz cumpleaños (p30)

Melody lines

27 ¿Adónde vas? (p32)

¿A - dón - de vas? ¿A - dón - de vas? ¿A - dón - de vas,__ mi a - mi - ga? ¿A -
a - mi - go?

- dón - de vas? ¿A - dón - de vas? ¿A - dón - de vas? ¿A un buen lu - gar?

FINE

Yo voy a Bar - ce - lo - na, Yo voy en au - to - bús.__
Yo voy a la pis - ci - na, Yo voy en bi - ci - cle - ta.
Yo voy a tu__ ca - sa, Yo voy, sí, voy a pie.__

D.S. (x3) al Fine

¡Sí, sí, sí! Voy en au - to - bús.__ ¿A -
¡Sí, sí, sí! Voy en bi - ci - cle - ta. ¿A -
¡Sí, sí, sí! Voy, voy, voy a pie.__ ¿A -

29 Tapas, patatas (p34)

Swing

Ta-pas,   pa-ta-tas,   gaz-pa-cho,   pa-e-lla,   Ta-pas,   pa-ta-tas,   gaz-pa-cho,   pan.

Ta-pas,   pa-ta-tas,   gaz-pa-cho,   pa-e-lla,   Ta-pas,   pa-ta-tas,   pan.

1.

'¿Qué   quie-res co - mer?'   'Un   he - la - do,___   por   fa - vor.'

'¿Qué   quie-res be - ber?'   'Quie-ro u - na   co - la,___   por   fa - vor.'   Me

gus - ta   el   pan   tos - ta - do.___   ¡Es   de - li - cio - so!___   Me

gus - ta___   la   li - mo - na - da.___   No me gus - ta___   el   ca - fé.

2.

'¿Qué   quie-res co - mer?'   'U - na tor - ti - lla,___   por   fa - vor.'

'¿Qué   quie-res be - ber?'   'Quie-ro un   zu - mo,___   por   fa - vor.'   Me

gus - ta___   la   en - sa - la - da.___   ¡Es   de - li - cio - sa!___   Me

gus - ta   el   a - gua___   frí - a.___   ¡No me gus - ta el cho - co - la - te!___

Melody lines

31 La Bella Durmiente (p36)

Ha - bí-a   u-na vez,   ha - bí-a   u-na vez,   Ha - bí-a   u-na vez   u-na prin-

-ce - sa.   Vi - no   u-na bru-ja,   Vi - no   u-na bru-ja,

Vi - no   u - na bru-ja,   muy   ma-la.   La prin - ce-sa se pin-chó, se pin-

-chó   un de-do,   Se pin-chó   un de - do,   la prin-ce-sa   dur-mió.   La prin-

-ce-sa dur-mió.   Diez,   vein-te,   trein-ta,   cua-ren-ta,   Cin-cuen-ta,   se-sen-ta,   se-

-ten-ta,   o-chen-ta,   No-ven-ta,   cien   a-ños.   Un

bos-que   cre - ció,   un bos-que   cre - ció,   Un bos-que   cre - ció   al-

- re-de-dor.   Vi - no   un prín-ci-pe,   Vi - no   un

prín-ci-pe,   Vi - no   un prín-ci-pe,   muy   gua-po.   Cor-

-tó   las ra-mas,   las ra-mas, las ra-mas,   Cor-tó   las ra-mas   con su   es-pa-da.   Cor-

su   es-pa-da.   Diez,   vein-te,   trein-ta,   cua-ren-ta,   Cin-cuen-ta,   se-sen-ta,   se-

-ten-ta,   o-chen-ta,   No-ven-ta,   cien   ra-mas.   Des-per-

-tó a la be-lla, des-per-tó a la be-lla, Des-per-tó a la be-lla con un

be-so. Diez, vein-te, trein-ta, cua-ren-ta, Cin-cuen-ta, se-sen-ta, se-

-ten-ta, o-chen-ta, No-ven-ta, cien be-sos. ¡Cien be-sos! ¡Cien be-sos!

33 Mi paga (p38)

Ten-go mi pa-ga. Voy de com-pras Un ba-lón, un C-D o

u-na con-so-la. Ten-go, ten-go mi pa-ga.

FINE

1.
'¿Qué quie-res?' 'Un ba-lón, por fa-vor. ¿Cuán-to es?' 'Son o-cho eu-ros.

¿Te gus-ta és-te?' 'Sí, es chu-lo.' 'A-quí tie-nes.' 'Gra-cias.'

2.
'¿Qué quie-res?' 'Un C-D, por fa-vor. ¿Cuán-to es?' 'Son quin-ce eu-ros.

¿Te gus-ta és-te?' 'Sí, es fan-tás-ti-co.' 'A-quí tie-nes.' 'Gra-cias.'

3.
'¿Qué quie-res?' 'U-na con-so-la, por fa-vor. ¿Cuán-to es?' 'Son no-ven-ta eu-ros.

D.C. al Fine

¿Te gus-ta és-ta?' 'Sí, es ge-nial.' 'A-quí tie-nes.' 'Gra-cias.'

Melody lines

35 ¿Qué tiempo hace? (p40)

37 El abecedario (p42)

39 El mundo es un pañuelo (p44)

Mi - ra el ma - pa del mun - do, Mi - ra el ma - pa del mun - do.

¿De dón - de e - res? De Gran Bre - ta - ña. ¡El mun - do es un pa - ñue - lo!

De Fran - cia ¡Fan - tás - ti - co! De Bra - sil ¡Muy bien!

De Mé - xi - co ¡Mag - ní - fi - co! ¡El mun - do es un pa - ñue - lo!

De Bél - gi - ca ¡Be - llí - si - mo! De Es - pa - ña ¡Ex - ce - len - te!

De Chi - le ¡Chu - lí - si - mo! ¡El mun - do es un pa - ñue - lo!

41 ¿Qué hora es? (p46)

¿Qué ho - ra es, por fa - vor?_ ¿Qué ho - ra es, por fa - vor? La

u - na, las dos, las tres, Las cua - tro, las cin - co, las seis, Las sie - te, las o - cho, las

nue - ve, Las diez, las on - ce, las do - ce. ¿Qué ho - ra es? A las

o - cho voy al__ co - le,__ A las nue - ve ten - go ma - te - má - ti - cas, A las diez__ ten - go

es - pa - ñol, A las on - ce co - mo__ un yo - gur._ Tic - tac, tic - tac, tic - tac, tic - tac,

Tic - tac, tic - tac. Tic - tac, tic - tac. ¿Qué ho - ra es?

Melody lines

43 La ropa (p48)

Dan-do vuel-tas, dan-do vuel-tas, Bai-la la ro-pa en la la-va-do-ra.

3rd time to Coda ⊕

Dan-do vuel-tas, dan-do vuel-tas. ¡La ro-pa! ¡La ro-pa! ¡O - lé, o-lé, o-lé, o-lé, o - lé!

La ca-mi-se-ta, La fal-da cor-ta, La go-rra ro - ja, El som-bre-ro. ¡La

⊕ CODA

ro-pa! ¡La ro-pa! ¡O - lé, o - lé, o - lé, o - lé, o - lé! - lé! ¡O - lé!

Number cards

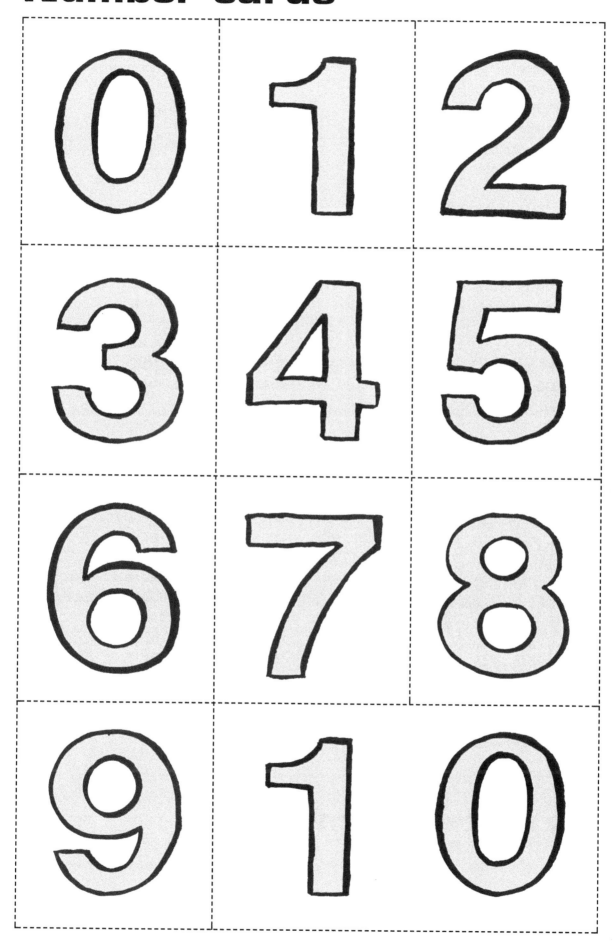

Track list

Track Contents

Track Contents

Teaching tracks

Spoken vocabulary to help teach key words and phrases

Track Contents

Acknowledgements

The authors and publishers would like to thank the following people for their help in the preparation of this resource:
Pablo Castillo, Fi Grant, Sheena Hodge, Hannah Hüglin, Jane Klima, Jocelyn Lucas, Lucy Mitchell, Uchenna Ngwe, Lucy Poddington, Cath Rasbash, Carolyn Reed, Jeanne Roberts, María Romero, Laura White and Emily Wilson.

Vocabulary and phrases in **La Bella Durmiente** used by kind permission of the Qualifications and Curriculum Authority.